Dedication

With gratitude to Wilma Henningsen Kelmer,
for a lifetime of love and encouragement.
LFP

To the preservation of the planet Earth
and to realize the end of global warming.
KG

Lori Peelen, Author

Lori Fisher Peelen lives in Northern California, with her husband,
her grumpy Saint Bernard, and two lazy cats. When she's not
working on kid books, she's usually rambling around in the
redwoods, or trying out new recipes on her good-humored family.
You can visit her website: www.streamriffs.com

Kathy Goetzel, Illustrator

Kathy Goetzel lives in Northern California. When she is not
busy working, she loves the chance to see her kids, gardening,
renovating her old house and dreaming up new art projects.

Reaching Halfway to Heaven

*California Redwoods and
the Logger Who Loved Them*

By Lori Peelen

Illustrated by Kathy Goetzel

Down Stream Press, USA

Prologue

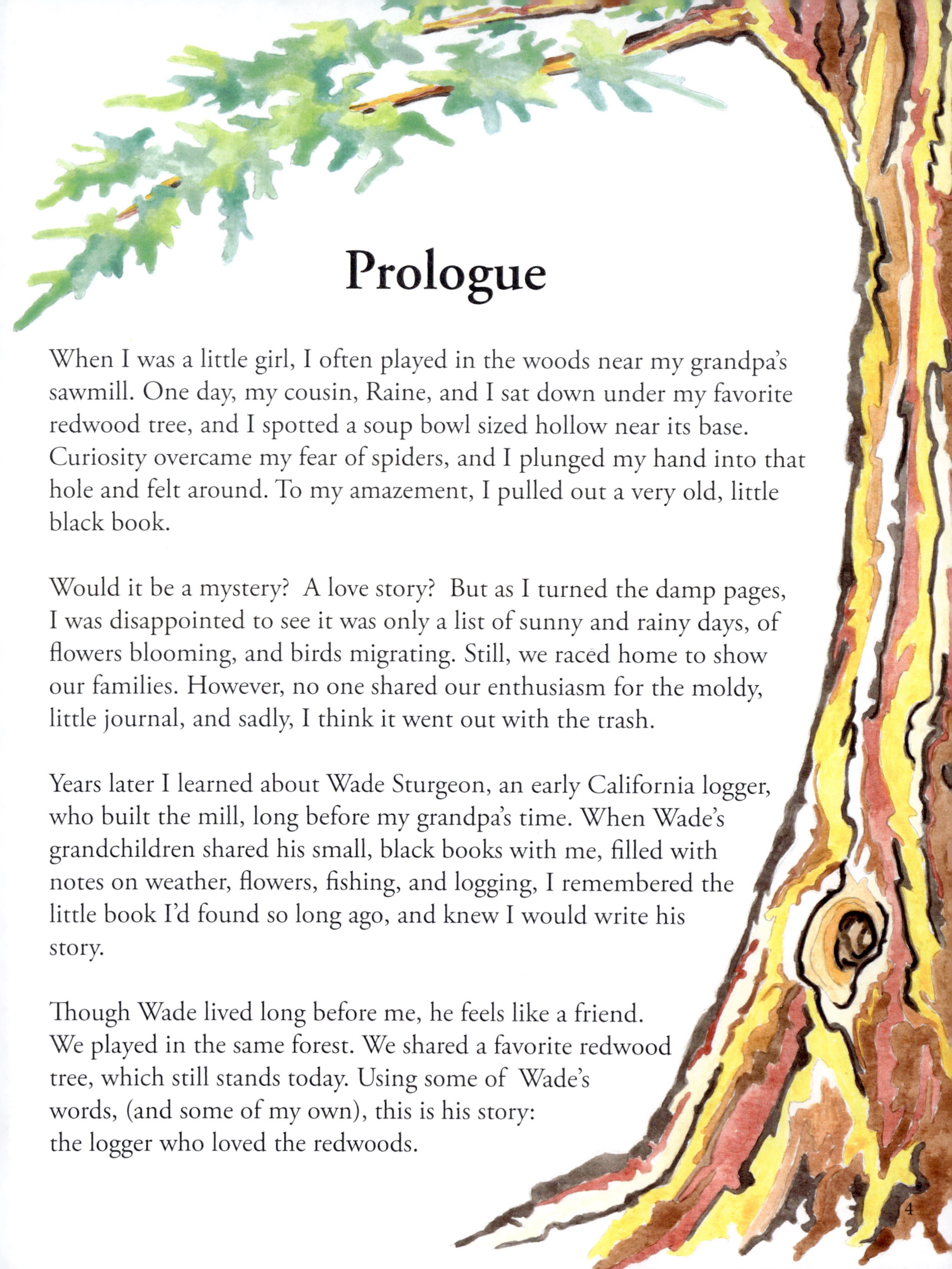

When I was a little girl, I often played in the woods near my grandpa's sawmill. One day, my cousin, Raine, and I sat down under my favorite redwood tree, and I spotted a soup bowl sized hollow near its base. Curiosity overcame my fear of spiders, and I plunged my hand into that hole and felt around. To my amazement, I pulled out a very old, little black book.

Would it be a mystery? A love story? But as I turned the damp pages, I was disappointed to see it was only a list of sunny and rainy days, of flowers blooming, and birds migrating. Still, we raced home to show our families. However, no one shared our enthusiasm for the moldy, little journal, and sadly, I think it went out with the trash.

Years later I learned about Wade Sturgeon, an early California logger, who built the mill, long before my grandpa's time. When Wade's grandchildren shared his small, black books with me, filled with notes on weather, flowers, fishing, and logging, I remembered the little book I'd found so long ago, and knew I would write his story.

Though Wade lived long before me, he feels like a friend. We played in the same forest. We shared a favorite redwood tree, which still stands today. Using some of Wade's words, (and some of my own), this is his story: the logger who loved the redwoods.

Growing up, redwood trees
surrounded me like friendly giants.
My sister and I built forts at their feet.

Redwoods kept me company while I dug up wild lilies growing in their shade, to plant in Mama's garden.

Their needles made a soft carpet beneath my feet, as I speared salmon beneath them. I liked fishing, but I liked learning about plants even more.

Wind in their branches sang to me as I wrote in my journal. I dreamed of going to college to become a botanist, to study all kinds of trees and flowers.

Hard times got in the way of my dreams. Pa died when I was still in grade school. Mama married again, but after a while, our new-Pa died too. Then, we needed money more than dreams. At fifteen, I packed away my books and went to work in the woods, to help my family.

Season after season, I grew stronger and taller, like my redwood trees. Now, I have a wife and two little boys of my own. Sundays, I tend the

garden around our little house. All week, I work in the woods. But come Sunday, I go to my garden, to plant new kinds of flowers and trees.

All my life, redwoods offered me beauty, shelter, and kinship. My needs are different now. My wife, Esther, needs a sewing machine. My little boys need shoes. My oxen need hay. For all these things, I need money.

Jobs are scarce here in the woods of
California, but redwoods are plentiful.
Redwoods can be cut into lumber and
sold for money.

This tree I've found is a giant among
giants, the biggest I've ever seen.
Ten men, with arms outstretched,
could not circle this redwood.

For two days now, my partner
and I have pulled back on forth
on this saw.

Pull...
        and rest.

I can hear my partner breathing hard on
the far side of the tree, but I cannot see
him.

Sweat drips from my forehead. Sawdust
tickles my nose and covers my boots.

Pull...
        and rest.

New blisters sting my calloused hands.
I'm a gardener, born to raise plants up.
Now, life calls me to hew them down.
It goes against the grain.
My heart hurts more than the blisters.

I figure this tree sprouted when
Jesus of Nazareth was a baby.

Pull...
     and rest.

It must have towered tall as a lighthouse when Miwok
fishermen paddled along the Pacific shores below.

Pull...
     and rest.

When electricity first lit up our little valley,
this tree already reached halfway to Heaven.

Pull...

and rest.

15

It pains me to take down this old giant,
but it will make good lumber,
straight and sturdy,
to build houses and bridges in San Francisco.

Finally, we take a break for water. I kick up
needles under the tree, searching for something
I do not find. I tip my head back to gaze at the
top branches. "I'm sorry," I whisper, offering
up a silent promise.

Somehow, some way,
I will help these trees that
have always helped me.
I pick up my end of the saw.

Pull...

and rest.

We have nearly cut through the trunk,
but the old giant does not fall.
It isn't ready to say goodbye to the sun, the sky,
and the birds in its branches.

I pound a wedge into the trunk, to help tip the tree.
I pound it in one inch…Two inches…The tree does not budge.
I feel my heart thudding hard.
Falling trees have crushed many lumbermen in this valley.

I keep pounding. Three inches…
Four inches…
At five inches, the old redwood groans.

A flock of doves lifts from its branches.
"Timberrrrrrrrr!" I yell, running backwards.
The tree smashes through others in its path with a mighty
roar, slamming into the earth. The ground shakes around us.
A cloud of dust rises. Then, all is silent.

I wipe my face and take a drink.
Crouching, I feel through the tangle of
branches, until I find the tiny treasure I
seek and shove it deep into my pocket.

All afternoon we chop branches off the tree. We strap
cables around the bare trunk and haul it down the hill.
It takes twelve oxen to pull this fallen giant.

My partner runs ahead, painting rough spots in the path
with bacon grease, to help the tree slide to the saw mill.

Finally, we arrive at the mill.
The sharp, clean smell of sawdust greets us.
White steam puffs from the engine.
Soon, a screeching, whirling saw blade slices the giant into lumber.
At last, the long whistle blows. Quitting time.

My arms ache, and my stomach rumbles,
but there is money in my wallet.
I drive my oxen home and give them
fresh hay and water.
I rub salve on their shoulders, where the
harnesses chaffed.

The smell of stew and biscuits welcomes me
at the door.
Dogs bark, footsteps pound, voices yell:
"Papa's home!"
I toss my little boys in the air.

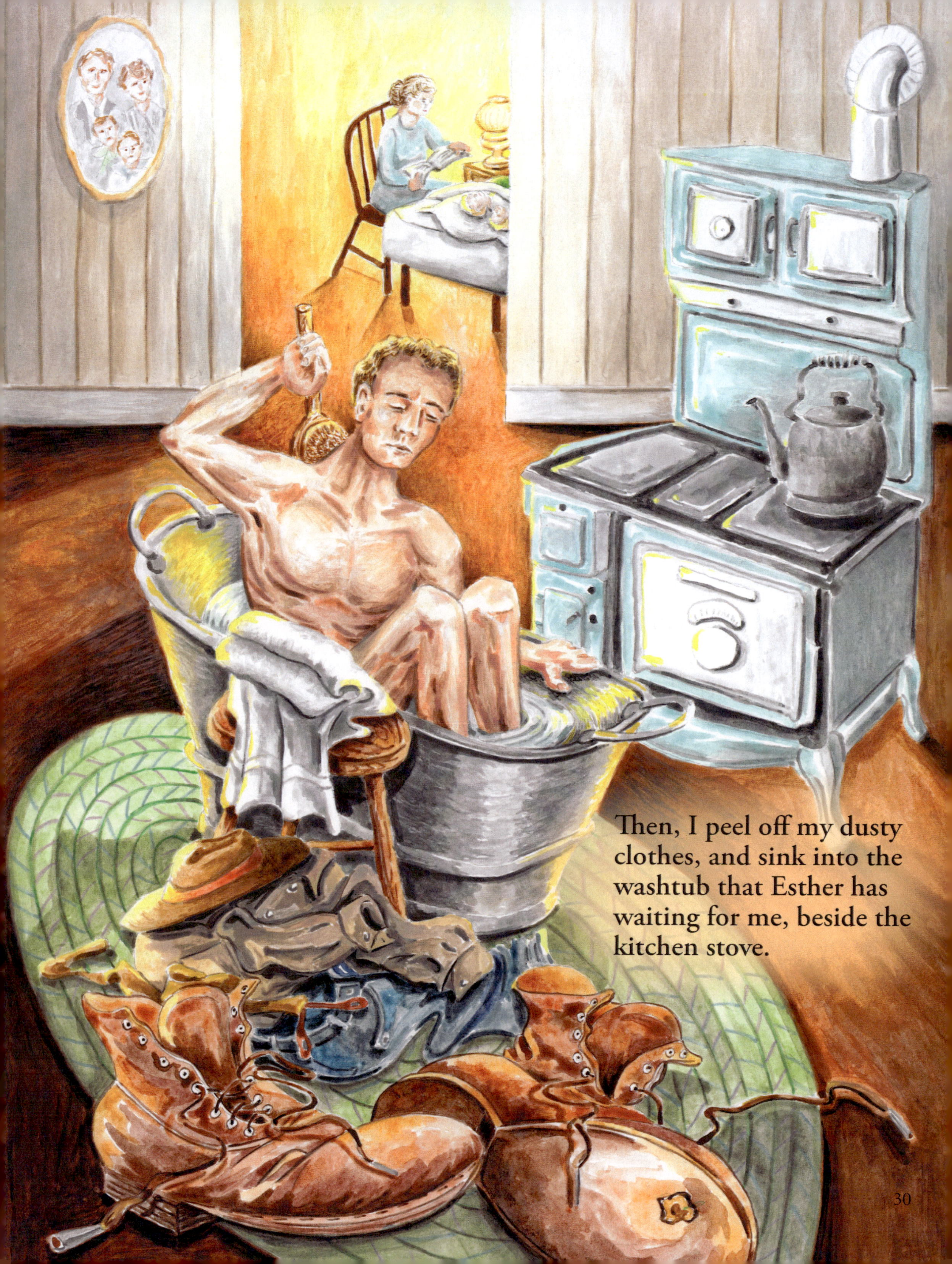

Then, I peel off my dusty clothes, and sink into the washtub that Esther has waiting for me, beside the kitchen stove.

At supper, we bow our heads to give thanks. I'll need to find another tree tomorrow, but for tonight, my family is sheltered, warm, and fed.

I write a few words in my journal.
"Dropped our biggest tree yet today.
A fellow gets pretty tired by evening.
Weather, fair. Mountain lilies beginning
to bloom."

Before falling into bed, I empty my pockets.
I hold the redwood cone in my hand.
I will keep my promise.
Come Sunday, I'll tap out the tiny seeds,
and plant them in pots in my windowsill.

I hope one day they'll reach *all* the way to Heaven.

Epilogue

Now that I'm all grown up, I see that Wade's journal was both a love story and a mystery. The love story was between a logger and his forest. The mystery is why he put one of his journals inside the heart of a redwood. I've gone back to that hollow many times, peering into the dark with a flashlight. But if there's something else inside, it's buried too deeply to see.

Our Friendly Giants

Redwood trees *are* giant. They are the tallest trees on earth, some over 350 feet high. Scientists estimate some of the largest weigh in around 4 million pounds.

Redwood trees are among the oldest living things on earth. Some have lived 2,500 years or more and are still growing! The Latin name for Redwoods, Sequoia Sempervirens, means "always green," or "forever living," because if a redwood tree falls, or is cut down, it sends up new baby trees around the old stump. This new circle of trees is called a "fairy ring."

Redwood trees offer shelter. Branches on very old redwoods are wide and twisty. Dirt and debris pile up there, making platforms in the sky. All kinds of plants take root here, even full-grown trees. These "forests in the sky" offer safe shelter for many animals, amphibians, birds, and insects.

Redwood trees share. Through their root system, redwoods share water and nutrients with neighboring trees, and send warnings of disease and danger.

Redwood trees are one of our best allies in the fight against global warming. Like all trees, they breathe in the CO_2 that we don't need, and breathe out the pure oxygen we do need. Because they grow so large, they can sequester more carbon dioxide than almost any living thing on earth, keeping our planet cool and comfortable.

Redwood trees live mainly along the Northern Coast of California and the Southern coast of Oregon. Only five percent of the oldest giants survived the logging exploits which began in the mid 1800's. Compared to the old giants, most of the redwoods we see today look like weeds. But these will grow, if we protect them.

Redwoods need our friendship and protection. You can help look out for these friendly giants, by learning all you can about what they need to grow. Make sure to visit them when you can. You will never meet a friendlier giant!

Lesson Plans and Study Guides for Teachers

- Redwood Curriculum, www.savetheredwoods.org
- Redwood Ed, A guide to Coast Redwoods for Teachers, www.parks.ca.gov
- Famous Trees, Homeschool Lesson plans, www.literaryhomeschool.com

Resources:

- *Wade Sturgeon's Journals,* 1906- 1949
- *Secrets of Old Growth Forest,* David Kelly, Gary Graasch
- *The Ever-Living Redwood Tree,* life and times of a Coast Redwood, Linda Vieira
- *Best Way to Fight Climate Change,* Forbes, July 2019, Trevor Wace
- www.savetheredwoods.com
- *Climbing the Redwoods,* Richard Preston, New Yorker, 2/14/2005
- *The Forests of California,* obi kaufmann

About Sturgeon's Mill

Wade bought the mill in 1913 for $700. and moved it by wagon and a team of oxen from Santa Rosa to Coleman Valley Road, where redwoods were abundant. By 1923, that timber was gone, and Wade moved the mill again, this time by horse-drawn wagon, seven miles inland, to a redwood filled canyon outside of Occidental, California.

As he grew older, Wade began to see that the forests of giant redwoods were not an endless resource, and would disappear altogether if they weren't protected. He became a lifelong member of the Save the Redwood League and studied sustainable logging practices. Wade preserved a grove of trees near his mill and redwood cabin, where he and his wife, Esther lived all their days.

Wade never stopped studying plants. He became a self-made botanist, and created a beautiful garden, that people visited from all over the world.

In 1943, Wade retired and sold the mill to his son, Ralph Sturgeon and Ralph's high school friend, Jim Henningsen, my grandfather. Sturgeon and Henningsen ran the mill until steam-powered saws were replaced by diesel engines and electric motors in 1964, forcing the mill to shut down. Ralph passed his portion of the mill to his son, Bob, and Henningsen passed his portion to his son, Harvey. In 1992, Harvey founded the Sturgeon's Mill Restoration Project, and Bob, along with five historians, joined the restoration project. Each member tossed in $100. to commit to the repairs… the exact price of the original mill.

Today, you can visit this living history museum, watch old methods of milling lumber, hear the steam whistle blow, smell the sawdust, and tour the gardens. Wade's beautiful botanical garden drew visitors from around the world. You can still visit it today.

For information on demonstration dates and how you can support this historical treasure, visit www.sturgeonsmill.com

Wade
estimate 1880

Wade
estimate 1883

Highschool Portrait of Wade and Esther
estimate 1896 • Occidental, CA

Wade and Esther's Wedding Photo
1905

Wade and Esther's Children
estimate 1913

**Esther Sturgeon in front of their house
near Occidental, CA**

Esther with their lilies
1933

**Wade and Esther Sturgeon's
50th Wedding Anniversary**
June 1955

Wade Sturgeon
1878-1957

Acknowledgments:

Kathy Goetzel, illustrations
Veronica DeCoster, editing
Rosalina Wilson, copyediting
Paula Pierce, editing
Katharine Cameron, layout design
Central Coast Kiddie Writers, critique
Harvey Henningsen, mill historian
Bob and Lavonne Sturgeon, journals and photos
Sylvia Fisher, my beautiful mom, a long-time docent at
Sturgeons' Mill, who encouraged this story

Cover and interior illustrations by Kathy Goetzel
Layout design by Katharine Cameron

ISBN # 979-8-9884558-0-6
Library of Congress # 2023915634

     Down Stream Press, Occidental, California

www.ingramcontent.com/pod-product-compliance
Lightning Source LLC
Chambersburg PA
CBRC090747110726
48005CB00008B/988